# How to Trust God -

# When everything goes wrong

"Your Promises Depends on It"

**By** JACQUELINE GORDON CAIN

# How to Trust God -

# When everything goes wrong

## "Your Promises Depends on It"

### By  JACQUELINE GORDON CAIN

©2014 by Jacqueline Cain Ministries
Printed in the United States of America

Scriptures quotations marked N.I.V. and K.J.V. (The New International Version and King James Version) Amplified Bible (AMP), New King James Version, NKJV, copyright ©1980, 1982, by Thomas Nelson, Inc. Publisher

ISBN:13: 978-0615955094 ISBN-10: 0615955096

Jacqueline Cain
MINISTRIES

Dear Friend,

I pray that this book will be a blessing to you and help you through the challenging times that you may be going through right now.  Know that this too shall pass.

With Love and Blessings

*Jacqueline*

**Jacqueline Cain Ministries**
**P.O. Box 891**
**Snellville, GA 30078**
**www.howtotrustgod.com**

For information about speaking engagements, visit the website: www.jacquelinecain.org.

# Acknowledgment

I dedicate this book to my beautiful family. Lee, you are the best husband a woman could have. You have prepared and provided for our children and me through these tests without a single complaint. I am blessed to call you, my husband. The favor of God has shined down on us through you.

To my children, Kia (Kim, Pierre, Kamden), Christiana, and Christin, thank you for going through the loss of your sister and the battle that your mother has been fighting with a smile. I feel blessed that you are my children. God knew that I needed my babies' love, and you have given that to me.

Friends and Hope and Life Church Family, thank you for looking out for my family and making sure we had what we needed. God's blessings on your family.

(Back Cover Picture- Day Melonie was buried)

Special thanks to Caryn Lott for making this book "readable!"

# Introduction

Jacqueline shares the critical principles given to her by God when she buried her 23- year- old daughter and had a double mastectomy because of Breast Cancer 10 days apart. She had to trust God, and He restored her hope and life. Jacqueline is the wife of Lee C. Cain and the mother of three beautiful daughters on earth- Marquita ("Kia"), Christiana, Christin Elizabeth, and one beautiful daughter and handsome son, Melonie and Jeremy in heaven.

# Table of Content

## CHAPTERS

1. Peace ...........................7
2. Being...................…..... 21
3. Testing .........................30
4. Change the
   Atmosphere/Surroundings.38
5. Mindset/Keep Walking.….43
6. Restoration and Favor ..…..51
7. Prayers......................54

# CHAPTER 1

# PEACE

As children of God, we must stay connected to Him to get relief from life issues and tests. You need a passport to obtain permission to go and come from the land that you were born. Just like you need a passport to have access to your rights as a citizen of the country that you live, you need a passport to be able to live and take advantage of the means that are provided to you by your country. We need a passport to the Kingdom of God to access our blessings. Without permission and connection to the Kingdom of God, you will continue to be a victim of life.

As children of God, we often forget to stay connected to the one who has control over our being. God created us and, therefore, is aware of every part of our nature. We often lose ourselves in the "Clutter of Life," just trying to make things happen in our lives. We put focus on what

is going on around us and less time talking and praying to our God. He will give you the shortcut to making sure you get your blessing on a timely basis if you stay connected to Him.

The Clutter of life started when we were born. We had to adapt to the world around us. Whether we had good, mediocre, or excellent parents, we had to adapt to their way of life and the lives of those in our neighborhoods, schools, churches, and workplaces.

Some of us were raised to believe in God and follow His laws, and others were not. It does not matter to God when and how you came to Him. What matters is how we choose to live our lives in a way that glorifies God's Kingdom and how we shine a light for others to follow the will and calling to become a child of God.

We need to inventory our situation to see why our blessings are not coming to pass and ask God for directions to break this hold on your blessings and quick release from tests.

The scriptures state that we do not war against flesh and blood, which means each other, but we fight against the things that we cannot see in the flesh. These things are taking place behind the scenes. This war can delay your getting answered prayers or impact how your blessings come. When this happens, your faith becomes weakened to the point that you have lost all trust in our God.

This booklet will teach you how to restore and teach you how to trust God and walk in victory every day.

The Lord took me on this journey on January 17, 2013, when on my 48th birthday, I learned that I had Breast Cancer, and on January 30, 2013, I was told by a doctor that my 23-year-old daughter, Melonie, was dying from Renal Failure.

Here we are nine months from the day that I lost both of my breasts and buried my dear Melonie, when the Lord came to me as clear as day and said, "I have allowed you to go through this to teach my people to trust me."

I now have my mission in life, and I have never felt more close to God than I do right now. I trusted that He would show me the rea-

son and meaning behind allowing my life to be turned upside down in a matter of 2 months...I had no control, and this was evident.

I pray that you take the right notes from this booklet and share it with all of those who need an extra dose of faith to continue to walk in the middle of "Life Changes."

The steps listed in the booklet were given to me by God, and I followed them to the "T" as I trusted Him and leaned not on my understanding of what was happening. Instead, I focused on Him and kept my mind off of the negative thoughts, people, and things that were in place (Clutter of Life) to take me down.

# Pain and Peace

*John 14:27*

*New King James Version (NKJV)*

*27 Peace I leave with you, My peace I give to you; not as the world gives do I give to you. Let not your heart be troubled, neither let it be afraid.*

None of us are excused from pain. We are excused from allowing the pain to destroy who we are and what God has planned for us.

There were days during my battle/test that I thought, "Am I dreaming?" Then there were days that I could walk into a room with a smile on my face, while everyone around me was waiting for the other shoe to drop. I knew that I had to stay connected to God to continue to stand. These tests were too hard for me to handle on my own. If you noticed, I said, "These tests" because I had my health and the death of my child happen to me at the same time.

The first thing that one should do is ask for "PEACE."

*John 14:1*

*Amplified Bible (AMP)*

*14 Do not let your hearts be troubled (distressed, agitated). You believe in and adhere to and trust in and rely on God; believe in and adhere to and trust in and rely also on Me.*

I immediately asked Jesus for "Peace."

He knew I was afraid, angry, hurt, confused, and that I felt abandoned. I am His child. No one should go through this much pain at one time, but God had a plan for my pain.

There was no way I could have made it through the night without asking God for "Peace." I was dealing with having to have my breasts removed due to Breast Cancer, but my baby, are you kidding me? No parent should have to bury their child. While all this was happening, I was thinking ..this is not how the world script should go. In the natural world, parents do not have to bury their kids. We do not live in the natural world only; we live in a spiritual world also.

*Hebrews 13*

*Amplified Bible (AMP)*

*13 And again He says, My trust and assured reliance and confident hope shall be fixed in Him. And yet again, Here I am, I and the children whom God has given Me.*

As a natural man, I need guidance from God. We were all made in His image for a reason. God made us in His own/likeness/makeup/DNA of God. We must stay connected to Him at all times if we are going to be successful in all things.

*Genesis 1:22*

*Amplified Bible (AMP)*

*22 And God blessed them, saying, Be fruitful, multiply, and fill the waters in the seas, and let the fowl multiply in the earth.*

The simplest way to explain it would be...I wanted to learn how to drive a car, so I watched my Dad and every person that drove me around. Then when it was my time to learn, I relied on my teacher to teach me all the rules of the road and how to stay safe. I could not have learned without keeping myself attached to the idea, need desire, and personalized teaching.

We, as people of God, must stay in tune with the plans and positions that God has designed for us. We were developed in God's heart way before we were born. Therefore, He knew what we would have to endure in this life; that is why we need to be in constant PEACE as He makes things right in our lives.

We must trust God to move us through life's challenges because He has designed our lives and the world from the very beginning to the very end.

Our earthly parents were the vessels used by God to get us here, but God is the Master Designer who allowed our parents to raise us. That is why we have learned to trust in people for our needs instead of God. Knowing that nothing just happens and that God is in control of everything, we must train our hearts to trust God and not man for our every need.

Jesus knew we would have the challenges and problems that we are dealing with and will deal with in the future. He knew you needed PEACE for your situation. Therefore, you have to activate your help by asking for PEACE.

Without PEACE, it will be difficult for you to stand...ask now for PEACE.

*Isaiah 26:3-4*

*Amplified Bible (AMP)*

*3 You will guard him and keep him in perfect and constant peace whose mind [both its inclination and its character] is stayed on You, because he commits himself to You, leans on You, and hopes confidently in You.*

*4 So trust in the Lord (commit yourself to Him, lean on Him, hope confidently in Him) forever; for the Lord God is an everlasting Rock [the Rock of Ages]*

# ASK FOR

# PEACE

## Galatians 5:22-23

### New King James Version (NKJV)

*22 But the fruit of the Spirit is love, joy, peace, longsuffering, kindness, goodness, faithfulness, 23 gentleness, self- control. Against such, there is no law.*

Hard situations are not too hard for God. Peace is one of the fruits of the Spirit, so ask God for it because it will be tough to stand in the middle of a test without it.

God laid it upon my heart that my situation was too hard to handle by myself, which are worrying, crying day and night, not eating, not sleeping, talking about it until people wanted to avoid me, and just being depressed.

This was not the solution!

I knew that this **"TEST"** was too big for me, so the only source that I had was my God. My husband could not fix it; my pastors could not fix it, nor could I fix it. My God was IT!

I am blessed and highly favored because a test this big was allowed to come into my house; it had to be permitted by the Lord. The enemy cannot touch a hair upon my head without God's approval because I belong to Him. The statement above should send chills down your spine...you belong to God. The quickest way to get relief is to ASK Him for deliverance.

Knowing that this "Test" was allowed in my life, I decided to hand it over to the Lord and leave it there.  I made it up in my MIND to let God fix the problems in my life and to keep my hands off of it or not expect others to fix it.

I prayed for "PEACE." My prayer was...."OK, Lord, since you are allowing me to go through this, you must give me **MAJOR PEACE** to be able to stand and not faint."

After I said this prayer aloud, while my husband looked on, I immediately felt the PEACE of God come over me and a calmness that I cannot explain with words.

I am not telling you something that I heard. I am letting you know the secret to moving through the difficult tests; which will help you to maintain your Godliness while keeping a SOUND mind.

I remember my Grandmother always said, "I am grateful because the Lord allowed me to wake up in my right mind." I now understand what my Grandmother was saying. When you go through life's challenges, it is critical to maintaining a "Right/Sound Mind," meaning sane.

Again, God never said that we were exempt from pain, nor did He say we would never experience pain. He said that He would always make a way out if we trusted Him.

While I was going through this pain, I put on my praise music. I couldn't sing with the music because my heart was so broken, but I listened and let my spirit talk with the Lord and allowed Him to count my tears and plan my escape. He already knew what I was thinking and feeling; I just needed to be...

*Psalms 69:29-31*

*Amplified Bible (AMP)*

*29 But I am poor, sorrowful, and in pain; let Your salvation, O God, set me up on high.*

*30 I will praise the name of God with a song and will magnify Him with thanksgiving,*

*31 And it will please the Lord better than an ox or a bullock that has horns and hoofs.*

I was holding on to a prayer of PEACE, while my head and heart played catch up with the Lord's plan.

I needed the Lord to restore Zion (Stability) in my life. The normalcy in my life had been taken from me in a blink. No more breast, no more Melonie, what does one do to keep standing? I just grieved and held onto His peace.

Sometimes as children of God, we think that we are excused from pain and trouble. The truth is, God's people deal with more challenged and more pain and stress than the unbeliever; because Satan has them in the bag already. The enemy wants us to give up and follow him, instead of holding on to God.

If you look back at your life today, I am sure you can see how some of the pain and trouble in your life made you a better person. What doesn't kill you will make you stronger.

Therefore, people of God, don't just pray that the Lord will keep the trouble away from your house but pray that if He allows tests to come, He will always make a way out and to keep you in perfect PEACE at all times, no matter what is happening.

# CHAPTER 2

## BEING
## The 2nd lesson would be:

# Just BE...

*Isaiah 41:10-12*

*(Amplified Bible (AMP)*

*10 Fear not [there is nothing to fear], for I am with you; do not look around you in terror and be dismayed, for I am your God. I will strengthen and harden you to difficulties, yes, I will help you; yes, I will hold you up and retain you with My [victorious] right hand of rightness and justice.*

*11 Behold, all they who are enraged and inflamed against you shall be put to shame and confounded; they who strive against you shall be as nothing and shall perish.*

*12 You shall seek those who contend with you but shall not find them; they who war against you shall be as nothing, as nothing at all. I know it is challenging for the average person to just go with the flow. Most of us have it in our DNA to worry. I was one of those people.*

*John 14:27*

*Amplified Bible (AMP)*

*27 Peace I leave with you; My [own] peace I now give and bequeath to you. Not as the world gives do I give to you. Do not let your hearts be troubled, neither let them be afraid. [Stop allowing yourselves to be agitated and disturbed, and do not permit yourselves to be fearful and intimidated and cowardly and unsettled.]*

I could WORRY, DAY AND NIGHT. I was a professional worrier instead of a warrior. If you change the letter (e) in the word "Worrier" to (o) in the word "Warrior," it means a different thing. We must war against trouble, not worry.

Worrier -means to torment oneself with or suffer from disturbing thoughts, fret.

Warrior- a person engaged or experienced in warfare, soldier

We put too much pressure on ourselves daily by worrying about what-ifs. When you are going through something, don't try to hide it behind all the other things that are going on in your life or act as it will go away. Worrying is very deadly to your spiritual growth and your health; this is a BIG trick of the enemy.

Take one step at a time and just be still. Identify your fears, worry list, and pain. Once you have these issues listed, hand them over to God, and trust Him to eliminate them. There is a saying, "98% of things that we worry about never happen." So, why would we give away the peace of God, by worrying about things that will never happen?

**Make your list here... (Fears, Worries, and Pain)**

1.

2.

3.

4.

5.

6.

7.

8.

9.

10.

I can speak from experience on this topic. I am now 49 years old, and 98% of the things I worried about, never, ever happened. Worrying takes away the valuable time of peace that I replaced with anxiety.

When people want to know how you are doing, be truthful. I am "Trusting that God is going to fix it." Do not re-live the pain over and over again by talking about it to everyone that you see. Just remember a cake in the oven can't cook right if you keep taking it out of the oven. We sometimes tie God's hands, when we keep picking up our problems and try to fix them ourselves.

Leave the problem with the Lord and just be...

When your mind starts playing tricks on you, just remember, "I gave it to HIM (The Lord), and that is it......

I tried so hard to stay busy during these TESTS that I almost forgot what I was going through. I had to take 20 steps back and say...It is OK to grieve for the loss of your breasts and your Child. God understands and knows that your pain is great.

Deal with the loss, test, grief, disappointment, failure, and pain, one day at a time and don't try and hide from it.

Just being is an art that most people do not have. We are taught to fix what is going on in our lives. You will have to learn to feel the feelings and go with the flow of allowing yourself to walk through the pain. I said to walk through the pain....never try to run. Running from problems will put a band-aid on the situation; when you need stitches to heal from the inside out.

You will re-live these moments in a wrong way if you don't allow the Lord to heal you from the inside out. It is possible to turn your tears into joy and a testimony to bless others by walking through this test the correct way.

**The secret is not to allow that pain to overcome you by changing your thought patterns from negative to positive thoughts.**

Whatever you do, don't get too busy hiding or running from the pain that you set yourself up for future pain.

Be kind to yourself; you deserve it. Take a walk in the park, go on vacation, spend time alone healing, help someone, read a book, or just take a nap when you need it. Find ways to relax and allow God to show you His plan for the pain that you are in right now. It is essential to not put more pressure on yourself to be "Normal" when things go wrong.

Being "Normal" is being "Real" with yourself and others. I am going through, but the keyword is "GOING." I am down, but not out, I am saddened, but not dead.

Let the people around you know that you need time to heal, and JUST BE......it will be OK.

An excellent friend told me..."Jackie, let someone else be the Cruise Director for now so you can heal." Great advice...let someone else take the lead, and you rest.

I was in the car with my husband driving home and told him about a list of things that I needed to do and how bad I felt that my energy level was so low. I could not get all the tasks on my list done. He began to explain to me that I was my **OWN** enemy....."Who would be mad or hold a Cancer Patient accountable for needing rest?" He reminded me that I desire the rest

, and this was a real dose of revelation. I had a great excuse just to say no and focus on healing.

Denial is a significant thing that the enemy uses. If you don't accept what is going on in your life, you will begin to press it down and not deal with or learn from the test; it can cause the test to continue and never, never, end.

From that day on, I began to say no to projects, people, and stuff in order to get the needed time to "JUST BE......"

If you don't stop the freight train in your life, it will run over you and take you out.

Make a list of the "freight train" items/situations in your life that need attention. (i.e., Need to have a clean house ASAP, people taking all of your time, bill collector that need a returned call back to say..."I don't have it," bad eating habits, spending what you don't have, etc.) and start eliminating them one at a time and take a break to "Just Be."

**Make your list right here...**

1.

2.

3.

4.

5.

6.

7.

8.

9.

10.

Comments/Thoughts

# CHAPTER 3

# TESTING

You will find out that during your time of testing, you will be walking in a fog. FOG meaning -"Following Outside Guidance" because it is hard to see. But choose the right kind of FOG-Favor Of God. You cannot go through any test without the Favor of God.

When God has allowed you to be tested, (remember the devil can't touch you or your family without permission), you can become so foggy that you start to walk in denial.

**Test** means- how the present quality or genuineness of anything is determined to utilize a trial.

**Testimony**- means evidence in support of a fact or statement of proof that you CONQUERED something.

If you look at scriptures in the Bible, you will see so many different tests that the people of

God had to endure. You will also see the promises that came right after being tested.

*Deuteronomy 8:2-10*

*New King James Version (NKJV)*

*2 And you shall remember that the Lord your God led you all the way these forty years in the wilderness, to humble you and test you, to know what was in your heart, whether you would keep His commandments or not. 3 So He humbled you, allowed you to hunger, and fed you with manna which you did not know nor did your fathers know, that He might make you know that man shall not live by bread alone; but man lives by every word that proceeds from the mouth of the Lord. 4 Your garments did not wear out on you, nor did your foot swell these forty years. 5 You should know in your heart that as a man chastens his son, so the Lord your God chastens you.*

*6 "Therefore you shall keep the commandments of the Lord your God, to walk in His ways and to fear Him. 7 For the Lord your God is bringing you into a good land, a land of brooks of water, of fountains and springs, that flow out of valleys and hills; 8 a land of wheat and barley, of vines and fig trees and pomegranates, a land of olive oil and honey; 9 a land in which you will eat bread without scarcity, in which you will lack nothing; a land whose stones are iron and out of whose hills you can dig copper. 10 When you have eaten and are full, then you shall bless the Lord your God for the good land which He has given you.*

Unfortunately, the people of God who were asking to be saved from Egypt had a problem with complaining and not being grateful.

## Learn How to be released from a TEST quickly.

The Lord said, "Trust Me In All Things" and "Do Not Rely On Your- self" (Mind, Body, and Knowledge).

Once you identify that you have entered into a "Test," ask Him...."What Did I Do?" "What do I need to learn from this?" "Yes, Lord, you got my attention." When you immediately surrender to His ways and will, the healing and promises can follow immediately,

When He gives you the revelation on what and why the test has come your way, do your part to get a "Clear" understanding and starting the healing process.

If you need to "Repent," remove yourself from something or someone, or give up something, do it immediately. Don't be surprised if this Test happened for you to be a blessing for others.

He knows our hearts and our thoughts; therefore, be upfront with the Lord and confess your shortcomings and obey to be released from the **TEST ASAP**.

*Genesis 22:10-18*

*Amplified Bible (AMP)*

*10 And Abraham stretched forth his hand and took hold of the knife to slay his son.*

*11 But the Angel of the Lord called to him from heaven and said, Abraham, Abraham! He answered, Here I am.*

*12 And He said, Do not lay your hand on the lad or do anything to him; for now I know that you fear and revere God since you have not held back from Me or begrudged giving Me your son, your only son.*

*13 Then Abraham looked up and glanced around, and behold, behind him was a ram caught in a thicket by his horns. And Abraham went and took the ram and offered it up for a burnt offering and an ascending sacrifice instead of his son!*

*14 So Abraham called the name of that place The Lord Will Provide. And it is said to this day, On the mount of the Lord it will be provided.*

*15 The Angel of the Lord called to Abraham from heaven a second time*

*16 And said, I have sworn by Myself, says the Lord, that since you have done this and have not withheld[ from Me] or begrudged [giving Me] your son, your only son,*

*17 In blessing, I will bless you, and in multiplying, I will multiply your descendants like the stars of the heavens and like the sand on the seashore. And your Seed (Heir) will possess the gate of His enemies,*

*18 And in your Seed [Christ] shall all the nations of the earth be blessed and [by Him] bless themselves, because you have heard and obeyed My voice.*

I want to take you back to the beginning of this booklet...You must stay connected to the source/creator God to live and walk through TESTS quickly. Be quick to obey and surrender.

If you need to rededicate your life to Him or ask Him to be your Lord and Savior, do it now. Say this prayer of Salvation. "Lord Je- sus, come into my heart to be my savior. I receive you as my Lord and Savior, and today, I know that you died on the cross and rose again to take away my sins. I choose to live for you. Help me to become the person that you have designed me to be and help me to follow you and you only.  In Jesus' Name Amen.

I asked the Lord to show me why I was allowed to have Breast Cancer, and His answer to me was, it would not be "Unto Death" and that He will use this to help so many others who are given a clean bill of health when there is something terrible going on. My mammogram report was good just one month prior. During my monthly self-exam, I found a lump. I asked God...."Is it Cancer" and He said, "yes." It took me 3 Doctors, 2 Hospitals, and three months to get an accurate diagnosis.

I asked for His "**TRUTH.**" Even though it was excruciating to hear, I accepted what He said and started moving to completion.

Now for my Melonie dying, I also asked Him why, and His answer was..."It is time for her pain to end, and you will be able to take care of yourself." Melonie had Cerebral Palsy, and her body could not take it anymore. She had lived a good life even though she had some disabilities. My baby was tired, and the Lord knew it. I just wanted to hold on to her forever because parents don't bury their children.

I got my answers from the Lord right away and faced the truth; I asked what need to get done next and allowed the healing to start.

I had an option to stay in denial and become depressed, but I knew that this kind of test could have taken me out. I have three other children, a husband, and the Lords' work. My second chance was appreciated and welcomed during this test.

Continue to give Him praise; even if you can't speak a word, **just let your heart talk to him. Remember, this too shall pass if you don't stop right in the middle of the test.  GET an A+, on life's Test by Trusting Him.**

# CHAPTER 4

# Change the Atmosphere/Surroundings

Sometimes you have to change your environment to move forward, which is a critical part of the trusting process. If you are surrounded by negative people, places, and situations, you will have a harder time moving to the next level in trusting God.

Most people are on different spiritual levels. Some will not be able to understand your ability to praise God in the middle of this Trial/Test. It is not your job to make them believe that God is fixing your situation behind the scenes right now.

I remember people coming to the Hospice Center to visit with Melonie and me, and they would say, "Just keep believing that she will get out of that bed and walk," or they would send me text messages about faith and healing. I was cautious about how I explained to them that it is in Jesus' hands. I already knew that the Lord was going to take my Melonie to heaven. He told me this, three days after she was in the ICU unit at the hospital.

Lee came to take me home to get a shower, and I began to cry in the shower and asked the Lord to heal my baby. He told me, "Not this time." At that moment, I knew that my baby was going home to be with Jesus, and there was nothing I could do about it. I had to be selective in who I told this because I had several people looking at me as if my faith was too weak. I understood that it had nothing to do with my faith, but my God had spoken, and who can change the mind of God?

It was hard for me to stop taking calls from those who didn't understand the peace that I had. It was also hard to renew my mind daily with all of the negative people judging my faith.

Our environment influences us daily. You are having a good or a bad day can be determined by what is happening around you. Therefore, make good choices to protect your emotions from negative influences.

Most of us tend to follow the flow of action, whether it is good or bad. It is human nature to adapt to your environment and place VALUABLE emotions into the spaces where you are living.

It is CRITICAL that you evaluate your living arrangement and those that live with or around you, to make sure you are separating the good from the bad.

If you continue to allow your environment to be a negative one, you will become who you live with or association with at the time. Hanging with the wrong group of people can take you down faster than your test.

I had a friend who was so negative that I started being negative about everything and didn't know why. If I had good news to tell her, I could barely get it out before she had a story that she thought could top it. She never looked on the bright side of life; she only focused on what was negative. Therefore, I had to change our friendship to an acquaintance.

I had to change some friends and limit contact with some family members, to have a stable place to "Trust God," without the negative choir singing in the background.

The enemy will set you up to fall prey to wrong "thinking." I can remember going through this last test and allowing my thoughts of continued pain to overwhelm me. I began to look for the other shoe to drop at any moment, and have the doctor diagnose me as officially CRAZY.

It is true, the Lord knows how much you can bear; therefore, set your thoughts on following His lead and not the lead of people and situations around you.

We do not have control over anything, but we try so hard every day to make things happen in our lives. We should be asking the Lord for help in choosing the right people and surroundings to have in our lives.

This process is hard to do at first. It is imperative to release your- self from "Toxic" relationships that make it hard for you to focus on your promises.

**Toxic**- means to be affected with or caused by a toxin or poison, a toxic condition, having an effect of a person.

If you have any one or anything in your life that fits the description of "Toxic," start making the change today. You don't have to be cruel or standoffish... you need to remove yourself from harmful or toxic people gradually.

Like I said earlier, it will be difficult, but the sooner you start protecting your environment, the better. When people ask what is wrong, just say...."God is working some things out in my life, and I need time to focus." Keeping Moving....don't look back! Lot's situation was being fixed because his environment was toxic, but Lot's wife looked back and died. (Genesis 19:15-29)

Let them know that it is a God thing and not something that you just want to be doing. You will set the example that God has control over your life, and you have decided to allow Him to put your surroundings to fit the "**Next**" level that He is taking you. Changing the scene changes the Chapter in your life.

# CHAPTER 5

# Mindset / Keep Walking

You know that the mind is a powerful gift from God.

*I King 3:9-14 (Amplified Bible (AMP)*

*9 So give Your servant an understanding mind and a hearing heart to judge Your people, that I may discern between good and bad. For who can judge and rule this Your great people?*

*10 It pleased the Lord that Solomon had asked this.*

*11 God said to him, Because you have asked this and have not asked for long life or for riches, nor for the lives of your enemies, but have asked for yourself understanding to recognize what is just and right,*

*12 Behold, I have done as you asked. I have given you a wise, discerning mind, so that no one before you was your equal, nor shall any arise after you equal to you.*

*13 I have also given you what you have not asked, both riches and honor, so that there shall not be any among the kings equal to you all your days.*

*14 And if you will go My way, keep My statutes and My commandments as your father David did, then I will lengthen your days.*

The Mind is our thought process. The mind-reasons, thinks, feels, wills, perceives, and judges.

The job of the mind is mighty. Therefore, we must continue to connect with the right thinking and focus on staying lined up with the will of God.

There were days when I could only think about, "How could this be happening to me?" Then there were days when I focused on the peace that the Lord had given me. When my mind started to wander, I would bring it back into focus on the fact that God is supplying me with this unspeakable peace and to not block this peace from happening in my life by letting my mind wander in the wrong places.

This process is very reasonable. You will find it easier on some days to keep your mind in check, but it will take everything that you have, and that is OK...God knows that we are human and allows us time to regroup.

I remember sitting in the chair at the Hospice Center looking at my baby dying and singing the song, "Alabaster Box," or "Stand" by CeCe Winans and Donnie McClurkin. I had to **re-MIND** my- self that He knows my need, and if I keep standing, it will be alright.

Jesus is aware of every feeling, tear, pain, and disappointment that we have. That is why I did not need to continue to beg Him for relief....it was on the way, and that is why He gave me PEACE to be able to wait.

I like to say...."I am minding God's business in my life." This statement is so true; if you focus on minding His business in your life, He will mind yours. Take the time to pray for someone else or volunteer in the Kingdom of God, if possible. If not, just pray for others and watch how God moves in your life.

Stop allowing your mind to wander on all the wrong things. Keep it in check daily per the Word of God.

*Isaiah 26:3-4*

*Amplified Bible (AMP)*

*3 You will guard him and keep him in perfect and constant peace whose mind [both its inclination and its character] is stayed on You, because he commits himself to You, leans on You, and hopes confidently in You.*

*4 So trust in the Lord (commit yourself to Him, lean on Him, hope confidently in Him) forever; for the Lord God is an everlasting Rock [the Rock of Ages].*

I kept reminding myself that He has always provided for my family and me. I would look back on the things that the Lord had done, which helped me to renew my mind and faith.

I remembered the times when I needed a job and got it the very next day. I needed some help with providing for Melonie, and He would always send the help right on time, and the list goes on and on. Why would I allow my mind to think only on the negative or bad things, when the good always, always, outweigh the bad.

It can get pretty confusing when you are going through something. The negative mind; writes a script that focuses on the problems with an ending written without a great outcome. Our thinking process must start off positive in the AM. We should always start our day of giving praise to Him, which is the secret to getting your mind in check first thing in the morning. You will find that you need to do this often throughout the day to stay on point. Just say a little prayer..."**God, you are right, and I trust you with my all."**

I now understand how people can give up on life and go too soon. After being diagnosed with Breast Cancer, I had so many people coming up to tell me the worst stories and not thinking about how it was going to affect me later.

These people are good folks; they were not thinking about the effects that this negative stuff can have on my MIND first and then my HEART.

I could have accepted the fact that a lot of Breast Cancers come back, and I will eventually (finally, ultimately at a later time) die from it.

My story and faith are written by God and not by man.

I refuse to allow the enemy to use people and negative thoughts to enter my Mind and then take residency in my HEART where the believing takes place.

See... God and I have a covenant to allow me to live and raise my children, be a blessing to others, work in the Kingdom, and see all of my promised blessings come to pass. I can't see my blessings from the grave. Therefore, I am re-MINDED that He told me at the beginning of this test.. that it would "**Not BE UNTO DEATH.**" I had to keep re-minding myself in spite of the negative people and thoughts.

I also had to be re-Minded to keep walking. It was hard some days to get out of bed, but I knew that this trick was in place to get me into a deep depression.

I saw about four different Doctors while getting Breast Cancer treatment and all 4 of them suggested that I take some type of anti-depression, because, in reality, I should have been severely depressed. They thought that someone couldn't be going through this kind of battle and not need a little help to get through.

There is nothing wrong with taking medicine to help regulate your mental state; it wasn't an option for me because I had to battle this test with God only. If I needed it, I would have had no problem with taking medicine to stabilize my emotions.

I asked the Lord for a little extra dose of PEACE and a clear understanding of how to keep walking in the middle of this test. Everyone around me thought that these tests were too hard to handle in the natural.

I kept saying to myself...."He will never put more on me than I can handle; therefore, keep walking, and He will continue to open windows, doors, paths, and avenues, and bring me out of this VALLEY moment."

# Keep Walking...

*Proverbs 19:21*

*Amplified Bible (AMP)*

*21 Many plans are in a man's mind, but it is the Lord's purpose for him that will stand.*

What is stopping you from walking?  (Write it here and remove all obstacles)

# Chapter 6

# Restoration and Favor

When I tell you that restoration and favor will follow and overtake you once you have followed these simple steps on "Trusting God," it is true. My family and I are living proof of the goodness of God. He is restoring our family day by day.

How one comes from under such Tragedy of burying your 23- year -old child and having a double mastectomy in a matter of 10 days apart, can only be described with proof of how God will keep you.

I am now living in my 10th month since my Double Mastectomy due to Breast Cancer and the burial of my Melonie, and I still have the amazing PEACE of God.

What's stopping you from walking? (Write it here and remove all obstacles)

When God gave JOB a hundredfold for his loss, I now know this personally.

*Job 42:10*

*King James Version (KJV)*

*10 And the Lord turned the captivity of Job when he prayed for his friends: also the Lord gave Job twice as much as he had before.*

*Job 42:12*

*New King James Version (NKJV)*

*12 Now the Lord blessed the latter days of Job more than his beginning; for he had fourteen thousand sheep, six thousand camels, one thousand yoke of oxen, and one thousand female donkeys.*

I have taken ten months off from work since my surgery, and the Lord has provided checks in the mail every month, and my health restored. I wanted a new car and was able to get one and paid cash for it... God is working it out and restoring my world to a double blessing for my trouble.

Thank you, Breast Cancer, for my brand new Breast(s), which is just like the ones I had as a teenager. The

Satan couldn't take my joy and peace, nor could he take my life.

My heart is still on the mend for my little Melonie, but I am confident that the pain will grow less as I remind myself that she is with her Jesus and has no more pain. I now have my own personal Angel in Heaven.

My new mission in life after the test is to teach God's people how to trust Him in all things.

I anticipate that this booklet will become a bestseller in the Name of Jesus because it was declared and given to me as a mission by God to help His people.

I can't say that it was me who kept me, but I can say that it was indeed the Lord. I am only flesh and bones and wanted to fold in the middle of this test, but Jesus decided to have GRACE and MERCY on me. He kept me blinded to the reality that this test was as big as it was until now...because I decided to TRUST HIM.

# Chapter 7

# Prayers...

These are some of the prayers that got me through.

## Peace for the Test Prayer

In the name of Jesus, I come to you asking for peace in this time of testing. Dear Lord, let my heart not be troubled as I learn to "Trust In You." I know that you are the only one that can move me from this point in my life into victory; therefore, Jesus makes the necessary changes in my heart, mind, surroundings, and focus so that I can put this test in your hands and leave it there. I trust you, Jesus, and I need you to continue to give me Peace to handle this test. Fix it, Jesus...

In Jesus' name Amen

# Wisdom and Open Doors Prayer

In Jesus' name, Lord gives me clarity and wisdom to make the right decisions in my life, open the doors that need to be open, close the doors that need to be closed, but always provide provisions for the closed doors. In Jesus' name. Amen

# Healing Prayer

In Jesus' name, Lord, I asked that you bring healing in my household. Lord, let your anointing be so strong in my house, that it flows down from heaven into every wall and person in my home. Let your healing power make bodies, minds, finances, and spiritual growth whole and line up with your perfect will.

In Jesus' name Amen

Dear Brothers and Sisters in Christ, just trust God in His word to keep and protect you in all your ways. May God's blessing be in your home forever.

Amen

## Jacqueline

Visit my website for additional information and resources.

www.howtotrustgod.com

www.jacquelinecain.org

## Day Melonie was buried

## Me and my sweet daughters

## Day of Cancer Surgery –10 Days Later

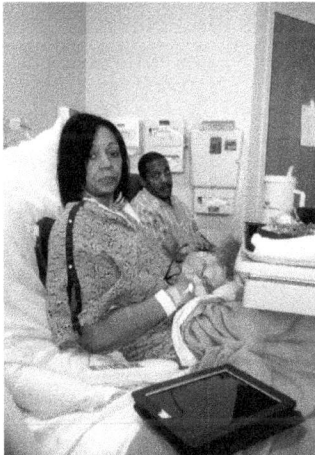